Self-Esteem

Conquer Feelings Of Insecurity And Enhance Self-assurance While Embracing Your Authentic Identity

(Tap Into Your Untapped Potential And Overcome The Confines Of Self-Doubt)

Mathieu Turner

TABLE OF CONTENT

The Development Of Self-Esteem And Confidence Over Time 1

Importance Of Self-Confidence 7

Acquaint Yourself With Your Negative Behaviors 29

Enhancing Your Self-Confidence And Excelling As An Introverted Individual 41

Enhancing Self-Esteem Enhances Decision-Making Confidence 72

Goal Setting Obstacles 78

Combining The Strategies 84

The Collaboration Between Happiness And Self-Recognition Is Mutually Influential. 93

External Validation 109

The Actions Of Others Serve As An Indication Of Their Character, Rather Than A Reflection Of Your Own. 117

Transformation Of Failure Into Triumph 128

Negatives Thoughts 138

The Development Of Self-Esteem And Confidence Over Time

The confidence in one's abilities stems from a complex interplay between innate predispositions and environmental influences commonly referred to as "nature or nurture." Within this context, 'nature' pertains to the specific environmental conditions in which an individual is raised, while 'nurture' pertains to the quality of care and nurturing they have received. Confidence is cultivated through a series of experiential milestones that enable individuals to thrive and achieve excellence. Henceforth, an individual has the capacity to cultivate self-assurance in numerous domains. Nevertheless, the advancement can be hindered by his self-perception. Therefore, placing utmost emphasis on self-esteem is of utmost importance in the domain of personality development.

"Investigating the Role of Nature and Nurture in Shaping Self-esteem

Home and relationship

Residence is the place where an individual initially cultivates their understanding of their own identity. The manner in which both parents handle their child is affected by the nature of their relationship. A child who receives respectful listening and communication from early on will develop the tendency to respond in a similar manner. He experiences a sense of acknowledgement, leading to the cultivation of a positive self-regard. Similarly, a child subjected to harsh criticism or neglect experiences the development of an inferiority complex, as they are led to believe that their actions and abilities are consistently inadequate.

Authority Figure

Individuals such as parents, guardians, educators, mentors, and significant role models exert a substantial influence on a person's self-worth. Commendation, endorsement, acknowledgment, recompense, and constructive response to errors made establish the groundwork for cultivating a robust sense of self-worth.

Likewise, sentiments of disappointment and insufficiency arise when a child is excessively exposed to unrealistic standards of flawlessness. Subpar academic performance, experiencing defeat in a game, or even minor errors made by an individual are construed as personal inadequacies.

Experience of abuse

Few things have as significant an effect on one's sense of self-worth as the encounter with abuse, whether it is of a physical, emotional, verbal, or sexual nature. In the absence of a robust network of support, he will inevitably become antagonistic towards himself. Bullying serves as a paradigmatic illustration of interpersonal abuse. The manner in which parents or guardians respond to a child's encounter with bullies significantly impacts their sense of self-esteem. A child who endures bullying within their household from their parents or siblings may perceive instances of bullying in other environments, such as school or elsewhere, as a mere continuation of their familial ordeal. It merely reinforces his conviction of being inept and ineffectual.

On the contrary, readily disregarding a child's traumatic encounter renders it challenging for the child to establish trust in others. On the opposite side of the spectrum lies an excessive inclination towards protectiveness. This does not instill in a child the essential principles necessary for his self-protection. Alternatively, he will continue to seek out a figure of authority who can provide assistance.

Belief System

This phenomenon is frequently associated with religious doctrines, particularly those that place excessive emphasis on personal deficiency, sins, culpability, and other pessimistic views of oneself. This phenomenon also occurs within collectives where individuals experience a sense of unworthiness in the absence of organizational backing. Extended exposure to this type of affiliation distorts an individual's perception of oneself. It fosters an undesirable reliance on the belief system and fosters doubt in one's own capabilities.

Media and Society

In contemporary society, particularly within the realm of media, an overly pervasive sway is exerted over individuals in shaping their notions of "goodness, beauty, and acceptability." Conventional standards have led to an understanding that physical attractiveness is synonymous with possessing an ideal physique, and the accumulation of material possessions is seen as the ultimate marker of achievement. As youngsters increasingly encounter the media's distorted depiction of societal values, they experience heightened feelings of inadequacy in the absence of conforming to societal norms.

Importance Of Self-Confidence

Self-assurance is the principal source of all other facets in your life. You derive from it in order to accomplish and establish the other aspects of your existence. Consider it analogous to the reservoir of energy that powers your existence. It is evident that the substance in question is not of a solid fuel nature; it cannot be simply categorized as a reducible substance, yet its existence is undeniable. It may go unnoticed by some, but self-assurance truly empowers individuals to succeed across all facets of their existence.

Career

Self-assurance is of paramount importance in your employment as, whether one likes it or not, organizations seek individuals with leadership capabilities. Upon perusing the aforementioned job advertisement, if one notices a preference for individuals seeking entry-level positions, it can be inferred that presenting oneself as an aspiring future leader will undoubtedly pave the way for success and advancement within that particular organization. Irrespective of the nature of the job for which you have applied, should the business enterprise perceive you as possessing the qualities of a potential leader, they would be inclined to make a considerable investment in your professional development. They would possess a considerable stake in fostering your personal growth. It is imperative to acknowledge that the success or failure of businesses heavily relies on their ability to efficiently transform ordinary employees into effective leaders.

Presently, this leadership role can assume an array of diverse forms. "You have the potential to assume the role of a frontline leader, which typically corresponds to that of a lower-level manager. One may acquire a position in middle management, or strive for advancement to the roles of vice-president or even chief executive officer. The outcome is contingent upon your actions and choices.

It is crucial to grasp the notion that enterprises are in dire need of prospective executives, primarily because the overwhelming majority of job applicants are driven by the necessity to meet their basic financial obligations. They are merely seeking to meet their financial obligations. They are not considering the long-term perspective; rather, they prioritize their immediate requirements, resulting in a limited number of them achieving leadership positions. It lies completely beyond the framework of their perceived role within the organization. They are simply striving to find a solution.

Should one possess self-assurance, the prospect of assuming a leadership role becomes attainable. It is feasible to envisage the accomplishment of tasks through the projection of determination and effort. You have the ability to motivate individuals, not solely through your efficacious output, but also through the emotive cues that you transmit. You have a tendency to inspire optimism in others. You have the ability to enhance productivity in a natural manner, as you serve as a source of inspiration to others.

These are the categories of individuals that enterprises seek to cultivate and elevate, as they possess the capacity to generate a sufficient number of leaders, thereby surpassing their rivals. Why?

The competition between them is fueled by individuals who possess highly transient mindsets. Those individuals are simply seeking to engage in labor in exchange for fair compensation. Nothing more, nothing less. In a corporation where none of the employees possess such a mindset, achieving significant progress is highly unlikely. It will perpetually be bested by corporations that possess capable leaders. Nevertheless, in order to assume a leadership position, it is imperative that you possess unwavering self-assurance.

Relationships

Interpersonal relationships inherently comprise of two distinct individuals, each possessing unique personalities, backgrounds, and histories. Whenever a disparity arises, it elicits intrigue, as there is no denying the exhilaration derived from conversing and engaging with individuals who have encountered profoundly divergent circumstances.

Although this disparity may elicit astonishment, it concurrently gives rise to discord due to disparate origins and backgrounds. You have not encountered the identical experiences; your upbringing did not entail the same ideas and influential factors. Hence, within the context of a romantic partnership, it is excessively effortless to perceive it through a lens of rivalry. Additionally, it can be perceived as a situation where one party prevails while the other party is at a disadvantage.

Regrettably, individuals with diminished self-assurance may easily be inclined towards an inclination wherein they deem it preferable to abstain from advocating for themselves and their needs, out of apprehension that doing so might result in the departure of the other party. To clarify, your relationship was influenced by your apprehension of losing them. At that juncture, the dynamic ceases to qualify as a relationship.

It is crucial to bear in mind that relationships serve as environments and structures that facilitate the personal development of both individuals involved. It can be challenging to make progress when one consistently deprives oneself. It is challenging to fully develop and flourish when one feels compelled to restrain oneself due to the fear of jeopardizing the relationship with the other individual. In the end, lacking self-assurance leads to the assimilation of your identity within the persona of your significant other. Put simply, the essence of the link pertains exclusively to their individualistic requirements, aspirations, prospects, and consequently, you find yourself compelled to contrive various justifications for allowing such a situation to unfold.

A prevalent justification involves self-deception, where individuals convince themselves that they are exerting maximal effort to sustain the relationship. You are not engaged in a discussion regarding the link since you are ultimately not involved in it. The correlation does not pertain to your significant other. Regrettably, during such instances, the nature of your support entails sacrificing your own well-being, desires, and personal identity within the confines of the relationship. Your sole focus appears to be on endorsing your partner, rather than extending support to others.

It is imperative that one maintains unwavering determination in their commitment to continue embracing love. It is imperative that you establish your own unique identity. It is imperative to ensure that your relationship is established upon a firm groundwork of mutual respect and equitable treatment. All of these prospects become unattainable in the absence of self-assurance.

In order for your relationship to thrive, it is necessary for you to receive recognition. The other party is required not only to acknowledge your presence but also to extend proper respect and value your input. In addition, they are required to occasionally yield to your authority. Put simply, you must ensure that your voice is effectively conveyed. Accomplishing this task becomes markedly challenging in the absence of self-assurance.

One additional rationale for the positive impact of self-confidence on relationships is the acknowledgement that perfection is an unattainable notion in the realm of personal connections. Individuals have the capacity to err, and indeed, they often do so. Either you or your partner may engage in acts of infidelity. One can inadvertently utter inappropriate remarks in inopportune moments, thereby causing unintended harm to one another. Numerous potential malfunctions and complications are possible.

In view of these circumstances, it is crucial to demonstrate perseverance. It is crucial to demonstrate resilience and resilience in the context of a relationship. There is no room for misunderstanding; your significant other possesses the capacity to articulate remarks that are incredibly devastating, piercing, and shameful, to the point where surrendering and departing seem like a natural response.

However, you don't. If the relationship holds sufficient value, one refrains. You hang in there. It requires resilience. It is imperative that you persevere until such time that you are able to effectively communicate in a manner that enables the individual in question to derive valuable lessons from the aforementioned sorrowful encounter, leading them to accord you the requisite level of esteem. It is unlikely to occur if you lack sufficient self-assurance from the outset.

It is highly plausible that your relationship may become exceedingly delicate due to the presence of low self-esteem, to the extent that it is merely a question of when one of you will eventually depart. If you perceive this task to be challenging, it is important to recognize that establishing a relationship necessitates a certain level of self-assurance. Why? Emphasize your uniqueness among competing candidates.

If your significant other possesses significant physical appeal or charm, it is highly likely that they will attract the attention of other potential romantic partners. It is contingent upon the extent of their attractiveness. Naturally, a heightened level of attractiveness or allure in a partner directly correlates with an escalated level of competition. Nevertheless, in the event that your partner does not possess the highest level of physical attractiveness, it remains a fact that there exists at least one individual who harbors an interest in your partner, or alternatively, your partner might manifest an interest in another individual. In order to differentiate oneself from the competition, one must possess a sense of self-assurance. You should be able to present a compelling argument to justify why your potential partner should choose you over others.

Life Enjoyment

When it comes to the aspect of quality of life, self-assurance plays a pivotal role. Truly, one cannot lead a life perpetually concealed from the public eye. If one lacks self-esteem, they succumb to becoming a mere countenance among the multitude. You begin to adopt the belief that your significance is considerably diminished. One begins to believe that their ability to express themselves is futile, as their voice holds no significance.

It is imperative to articulate one's needs in order to effectively navigate through life. Why? Individuals have the capacity and propensity to disregard your personal boundaries and undermine you. Indeed, life can be characterized as a competitive and ruthless environment.

Disregard all previous information that you have been exposed to. It does not depict a utopian reality filled with radiance, joy, mythical creatures, and sweet treats. The conditions can be extremely harsh in that environment. Regrettably, an excessive number of individuals tend to seize upon any signs of vulnerability and exploit them as opportunity to enter. Should you grant someone a small concession, it is not unusual for them to desire a substantial gain. If you assist someone, do not be astonished if they also seek your further support.

It is imperative to possess the capability to advocate for one's own needs. You must possess the capability to assert and defend your rights. One cannot simply reside in the shadows and consistently capitulate. It will impede your ability to derive pleasure from life. You sense that you are progressively compromising for something that is shrinking incrementally as time goes by. One begins to experience a sense of being a mere observer in one's own existence, wherein irrespective of one's thoughts, circumstances, and emotional pain, their significance appears significantly diminished. Notice the extent to which this is detrimental? Do you comprehend the manner in which you have organized your existence in a manner that leads to such a lamentable state? It is truly disheartening, considering your considerable potential.

In order to achieve success in any endeavor, it is imperative to possess unwavering self-assurance. It is not within anyone's capability to accomplish this task on your behalf. No other individual would undertake the task on your behalf. No one else possesses the capability to accomplish this task on your behalf.

Fostering an Optimistic Perspective for a Fulfilling Existence

Our overall perspective and demeanor towards life significantly shape our level of happiness.

within the course of our daily lives and the level of our efficiency. An individual who carefully reflects upon every aspect will

Display an escalating tendency towards relaxation, tranquility, and a greater frequency of smiling compared to an individual who maintains a constant vigilance towards their surroundings.

On the contrary, there are individuals who willingly allow themselves to be affected by pressure and consistently don a frowning expression.

Not only does the way you think and feel impact you, but it also has an impact on others.

In summary, our mental state has a direct impact on the trajectory of our day, within our proximity. Establishing and maintaining a source of motivation

Have a positive and fulfilling life necessitates adopting a particular perspective.

There are various methods through which one can cultivate a more positive mindset.

and begin to alter your contemplation of various circumstances that you encounter on a daily basis.

living. Maintaining a positive demeanor and refraining from indulging in negative thinking would necessitate certain adjustments.

Despite its gravity, in the long term, the fresh perspective will ultimately manifest as organic. The five pri

"Several key considerations to bear in mind when altering your perspective are:

1. Shift your perspective towards constructive reasoning and strive to engage in daily practice of empathetic thinking.

It is recommended that you focus your mental energy on completing each task sequentially, while solely contemplating a favorable outcome.

Indulge in the exquisite satisfaction that awaits once you have successfully completed the task. Never surrender to uncertainty

Moreover, allow yourself to acknowledge the substantial responsibilities you have assumed, while resolutely persevering. 2. Do not allow your conversations to take a negative turn, as it is quite easy to succumb to

Allowing others to undermine your morale, particularly if they hold a pessimistic viewpoint.

of view. Please refrain from being tempted to revert to your previous behaviors; instead, endeavor to convert pessimistic speech into positive discourse.

Maintain an optimistic mindset and actively seek out the positive attributes in everything and every situation.

3. Seek the inherent strengths and virtues within those in your immediate vicinity, prompting their elevation to the forefront of their being. By doing so, you shall

Create an atmosphere of inspiration and positivity around you.

4. In all aspects of your daily routine, endeavor to consistently seek out the positive attributes within it.

even though it may be a demanding endeavor that you typically despise and

When encountering a situation that elicits negative emotions, endeavor to find an aspect of it that can be reinterpreted in a manner that conveys a positive connotation.

a situation that is constantly improving in a positive manner.

5. It is important to always resist becoming preoccupied or deceived into reverting back to pessimistic thinking, as doing so takes considerable time and effort.

to alter your emotional and cognitive states, in the event that you have been

If you have been heavily critical, both of yourself and the world, for a significant period of time, it will take a considerable duration for your newly adopted perspective to fully take hold.

Enroll and linger in proximity.

Over the course of time, you will come to realize that various aspects of your life have the potential to be transformed by mere action.

Shifting your perspective from a pessimistic viewpoint to an increasingly optimistic one. Upon exploration, you will discover that your

As one's confidence grows, their level of recognition increases steadily, leading to a heightened sense of happiness and contentment.

Certainly, now you possess the capability to manage the tasks that previously provoked your displeasure without them inducing distress.

An enhancement of your connections becomes evident when you experience heightened levels of stress and nervousness. These are just a few of the territories.

Discover realms of personal development that empower one to cultivate a continuously motivating mindset, thereby fostering a more optimistic existence.

Acquaint Yourself With Your Negative Behaviors

Negative behaviors are manifested in one's nonverbal communication. If one possesses a propensity for indolence, they tend to assume a slouched posture frequently. Individuals who possess a predisposition towards falsehoods often exhibit a greater frequency of ocular blinking compared to their counterparts. Various interpretations can be drawn from one's body language, and in order to exude confidence, it is imperative to recognize and address any unfavorable habits, as they are not fostering a positive impression among others.

Do you engage in the habit of biting your nails?

In the event that you do, it will not go unnoticed by others. The intricacies of such matters are bound to be keenly observed by your interviewers. It is evident that your lack of self-confidence is quite apparent. It is highly advisable that you consider undergoing a treatment as a means of alleviating these behaviors, as it can significantly contribute to enhancing your self-image and overall well-being. Habits are exclusively formed as a result of consistent and repetitive behavior. Hence, whenever you find yourself proceeding to place your hand towards your mouth, engage in an alternative action of consistent nature, thereby enabling the substitution of the habit. Each instance in which you yield to it, you fortify the pattern. Nevertheless, in the event that you conceive an alternate course of action, compel yourself to undertake it. As an illustration, in the event that you observe the inclination to bring your hand near your mouth with the intention of nibbling your nails, I recommend grasping a pencil and jotting down a goal that you aim to accomplish within the current day. That is indeed an admirable practice to substitute a negative habit with a positive one. Once your nails have grown and their state calls for a manicure, you will experience a sense of satisfaction regarding the accomplishment.

You engage in excessive smoking.

Initiating tobacco consumption often begins as a communal practice. Nevertheless, in contemporary times, there is limited justification for the overt display of smoking. By consecutively smoking one cigarette after another, you demonstrate to those in your vicinity that you possess a predisposition towards anxiety. Might I suggest purchasing a pack of nicotine patches or opting for nicotine replacement chewables as an alternative means to supplement the nicotine intake typically obtained from cigarettes? The condition of your body is determined by how well it is cared for. Each cigarette you smoke contributes to negative self-perception and exacerbates the gradual deterioration of your health. Take pride in the utilization of alternatives. You will have a reduced impact on others and emit a more pleasant aroma.

One tends to engage in manual activity when experiencing nervousness.

When circulating within a space, endeavor to maintain your hands in a position adjacent to your body. When you take a seat, endeavor to replicate the action. If one is aware of the culpability associated with fidgeting with one's fingers, it would be beneficial to cease this behavior by tucking one's hands beneath one's thighs.

Focus on cultivating behaviors that indicate a deficiency in self-assurance. Below are a few examples that will aid your ability to identify such occurrences when they befall you. It typically requires an approximate period of 31 days to cultivate a commendable practice. Hence, upon recognizing the resurface of the old habit, substitute it with a positive habit, as doing so will contribute to the acquisition of greater self-assurance.

- Averting one's gaze when engaged in a conversation with someone.

- Casting one's gaze downward in a deferential manner

- Exerting pressure on your lower lip with your teeth

- Moistening your lips with your tongue

- Being in constant motion.

- Demonstrating excessive unease in articulating one's thoughts

- Demonstrating excessive dependency and seeking approval • Expressing a high level of neediness and seeking validation from others

Let us carefully analyze a select few of these elements, as their significance is noteworthy and can profoundly influence the perception of your actions by others. When an individual averts their gaze from others during a conversation, it conveys several possible impressions. It seems that you are either disinterested in listening to their perspective or eager to conclude the conversation promptly. To enhance your conversation skills, it is advisable to maintain direct eye contact with the person speaking to you and refrain from blinking. Look interested. Display an attentive and engaged demeanor.

Engaging in a posture of submission by casting your gaze downwards renders you susceptible to exploitation by individuals who will take advantage of your vulnerability. This phenomenon occurs due to the fact that specific individuals derive a sense of exhilaration from wielding authority, despite their awareness of its inherent constraints. Take bullies for instance. They derive pleasure from causing harm to individuals who express their pain. Should you persist in displaying an inclination towards submissiveness, you shall inevitably draw individuals of such nature towards your presence. Consequently, rather than appearing submissive, it is advisable to engage in the practice of maintaining an erect posture. Maintain direct eye contact and refrain from retreating when engaged in conversation with others.

Exhibiting a significant dependency on others and seeking constant validation is an undesirable behavioral pattern. How frequently have you communicated this to your superior?

Are you satisfied with the level of progress I have made today?

Was my performance satisfactory?

Do you believe that I will eventually comprehend?

The habitual phrases that you employ in an attempt to garner praise are fundamentally counterproductive. These behaviors indicate a deficiency in self-assurance and contribute to the exhaustion of those around you, as they would rather collaborate with individuals who possess the self-assurance to perform their tasks without relying on external validation. It is not customary to frequently encounter managers and CEOs soliciting such forms of authorization. They possess the knowledge of proper conduct." "They exhibit commendable manners and behavior." "They demonstrate a thorough understanding of appropriate conduct." "They are well-versed in the art of proper behavior." "They exhibit a keen sense of decorum and etiquette. Should you find yourself engaging in such behavior, it is imperative to commence the alteration of your linguistic expressions, thereby manifesting assurance and instilling trust in your ability to shoulder the entrusted obligations. Certainly, I will promptly address and complete the tasks assigned by my superiors."

"No problem. I will undertake that task subsequently."

"Thanks a lot. I am inquiring as to my scheduled activities for today."

May I request assistance from someone for this task?

One is not required to possess knowledge in every domain, however, acquiescence ought never to be deemed acceptable. Be happy. Strive to embody the attributes of an individual with whom you would choose to collaborate. Please keep in mind that within a professional environment, there is a finite amount of time available for completing tasks. If you anticipate constant commendation from your employer, such an outcome is not forthcoming. If such a circumstance were to occur, it would likely be attributed to an excessive dependence on others. Perform your duties diligently and with sincerity, and in cases where you are unsure of how to proceed, do not hesitate to seek clarification. Maintain amicable relations with your colleagues and refrain from bringing personal issues into the workplace. Bear in mind, it is possible that they are facing personal challenges, and your attitude of happiness contributes to brightening their days.

Enhancing Your Self-Confidence And Excelling As An Introverted Individual

Introverts possess distinct qualities that perplex many individuals who struggle to comprehend them. They can often be observed in the outer boundaries of most social gatherings. Their demeanor may be misconstrued as shyness, despite this being an erroneous assumption. Introverts have a limited capacity to expend social energy, hence necessitating periods of withdrawal and recharging.

In a society predominantly populated by individuals who are inclined towards extraversion, introverts may encounter greater challenges in their pursuit of professional advancements and social connections. However, it is more advantageous for them to remain within their introverted sphere, as attempting to present themselves as anything other than their true selves would prove arduous.

Numerous individuals with introverted tendencies benefit from receiving encouragement to enhance their self-esteem, thereby allowing them to authentically exhibit their true potential. Despite the inherent challenges, accomplishing this task remains within the realm of possibility.

Being an introvert is not a deficiency in character; instead, it is a characteristic of one's personality, comparable to being an extrovert. Western society tends to exhibit higher levels of extroversion and enthusiasm, while Eastern societies have traditionally shown greater acceptance towards introverted individuals.

Nations like China, Korea, and Thailand serve as sanctuaries where introverted individuals are not subjected to feelings of inferiority; rather, they are regarded as exemplary beings. The denizens of such nations hold the belief that exhibiting reserve and contemplation is praiseworthy and indicative of virtuous character.

There exist numerous avenues through which introverted individuals can display their talents and abilities with brilliance.

Adopt a constructive outlook on your personality - Embrace being an introvert without any sense of disgrace! It is not a defect, but rather a distinguishing characteristic. Introverts are not alone. Indeed, there is a higher number of individuals similar to yourself than your awareness presently acknowledges.

Refrain from engaging in self-criticism, and come to terms with the reality that you may encounter challenges in certain undertakings. Maybe engaging in conversations with unfamiliar individuals isn't your forte, and delivering speeches in a public forum, before a gathered audience, elicits an even greater level of fear than navigating through a haunted house. Recognize your weaknesses, irrespective of their nature, and refrain from excessively criticizing oneself.

Gain a comprehensive understanding of your introverted nature – Introverts exhibit a variety of personality types. The fundamental aspect of introversion lies in gaining renewed energy by engaging in solitary activities or by being in the company of a trusted individual who provides companionship and support.

An additional crucial aspect involves assimilating information prior to formulating a response. You are encouraged to carefully reflect upon the information that is being conveyed to you. For example, a person with extroverted tendencies might peruse an online article and promptly engage in active discourse, expressing their viewpoint on the subject matter. In contrast, it appears that you aspire to take some time aside for contemplation regarding the contents of the article before articulating your viewpoint. That is, if you choose to contribute any viewpoint whatsoever. There is the matter of privacy that you relish preserving, hence the likelihood of sharing your thoughts may be limited. (Boyes, 2013)

Every introvert is different. Consequently, you have the ability to derive valuable guidance from the information that is beneficial to you, while disregarding any irrelevant aspects.

Do not engage in comparisons with extroverts - Potential as an introvert, it is conceivable that you have envisioned yourself as the focal point, captivating the crowd at social gatherings. You hold the influential role of captivating the attention of others as you recount your most recent exploits during your trip to Australia, recounting the destinations you visited, the activities you engaged in, and the individuals you encountered.

Despite the apparent allure of being the center of attention at social gatherings, it is crucial to recognize the inherent merits of possessing introverted qualities as well.

As an illustrative example, consider the scenario wherein you have authored a highly successful novel that garners widespread acclaim, leading your publisher to duly notify you of an upcoming book tour. Would you derive satisfaction from undergoing numerous interviews and being constantly under scrutiny?

If you happen to be an individual with introverted tendencies, the aforementioned scenario may not be something you would prefer to encounter. If one truly identifies as an introvert, they would prefer to receive due recognition from a secure vantage point.

Embrace your true self - specifically, the individual endowed with a keen ability to decipher subtleties that surpasses those who garner greater prominence. (Hayward, 2018)

The distinction between a deficiency in self-assurance and having introverted tendencies.

Individuals who possess confidence exhibit a firm belief in their abilities and approach, coupled with a conviction that they will be favorably received by a majority of individuals. If one of these essential components is absent from your repertoire of self-assurance, it would be prudent to dedicate effort towards its cultivation.

Compose a blog post - individuals who possess introverted traits derive pleasure from solitude, as it allows them to reflect upon their ideas and meticulously transcribe them into written form. The contemporary realm of digital weblogs serves as an ideal platform for introverted individuals to articulate their thoughts and emotions.

Extroverts are often praised for their sociability, however, introverts can also make significant contributions through the utilization of social media.

Possessing a reserved disposition can contribute to the establishment of credibility. In our society, individuals who vocally express themselves with greater intensity often attract attention, whereas introverts, who possess the patience to observe and actively listen, devote their efforts in doing so. Hence, their observations can be consequently transformed into written compositions that genuinely resonate with the audience.

Exhibit ingenuity - Introverts devote a significant portion of their time to introspection, contemplating information and experiences they have encountered. As aforementioned, this ingenuity is conducive to the composition of a blog, and additionally, it has the potential to reveal other dimensions of an individual's character.

In general, individuals characterized as introverts tend to exhibit a greater propensity for creativity. Research has provided evidence to support the notion that individuals who identify as introverts possess a unique capacity to engage in their creative endeavors with a heightened level of deliberation compared to their extroverted counterparts.

The aforementioned studies also indicated that introverts have the ability to collaborate effectively with others, indicating that although you may not possess an inherently artistic nature, you can still contribute valuable ideas without overshadowing the input of other individuals involved.

Exhibit leadership qualities and act as a role model - As highlighted by the reputable publication Forbes, esteemed business leaders such as Bill Gates, the visionary behind Microsoft, and the immensely successful investor Warren Buffet, greatly value their solitude. Forbes posed the inquiry as to whether businesspeople who are quiet and reserved by nature possess the potential to achieve exceptional success in their own leadership roles within their respective industries.

The response, along with its accompanying rationale, can be provided as follows: Introverted leaders exhibit a characteristic of carefully deliberating before expressing their thoughts, prioritizing thoughtful consideration of others' viewpoints. Introverts additionally demonstrate heightened composure amidst a crisis, thereby establishing a standard for the staff's response.

A business executive who dedicates time to rejuvenate oneself can enhance their ability to effectively respond to challenging situations and approach them in a composed manner rather than react impulsively.

Minimize casual conversation - Introverts tend to refrain from engaging in extensive verbal interactions when establishing new friendships or building romantic connections. This may be erroneously interpreted as a manifestation of lack of interest. It is conventionally assumed that being amicable and sociable is necessary to initiate a conversation with an unfamiliar individual; however, it is also possible to delve directly into the topic of interest without engaging in preliminary chit-chat.

While it is indeed important to practice your small talk skills for smoother communication, it is also possible to directly address the topic at hand without circumlocution.

There is no essential requirement to discuss the current headline or the likelihood of precipitation. You may simply greet the individual by using the word "Hello." The dialogue will proceed from that point onward. There is an absence of fear and a minimal requirement of significant exertion to initiate the discourse.

Love interests require attention – Introverts encounter challenges when initially interacting with individuals. They maintain a state of tranquility and therefore convey an impression of detachment. In order to address this perception, it is advisable to communicate your introverted nature to the other party right from the beginning. They could potentially possess introverted tendencies, which might contribute to a heightened sense of relaxation on your date.

To facilitate the smooth progression of the conversation, one may also inquire about their travel experiences or their literary preferences. Inquire about the same matters that have been posed to you by your companion as well.

The purpose of the date extends beyond solely making a positive impression on the other person. One should ascertain their own level of interest during a date, rather than focusing on whether the other person is interested in them. Please bear in mind, the date should entail equal participation and involvement from both parties.

Acquire knowledge about the factors that cause excessive stimulation – outlined below are several instances: receiving inquiries and requests for decisions while concentrating on a thoughtful response, experiencing frequent disruptions, exposure to loud environments, engaging in continuous social interactions, attending group meetings, and utilizing various social media platforms - encompassing all of these situations.

Seek to reduce and discover techniques to circumvent any stimuli that may trigger excessive arousal in your system. Learn physiological self-regulation tactics. (Boyes, 2013)

Physiological Self-Regulation Tactics
These strategies of self-regulation have the potential to facilitate the alleviation of stress. The efficacy of their operations

is substantiated by renowned psychologists.

There is no need for you to excel in every aspect. Nevertheless, endeavoring to make progress can still be advantageous. The pursuit of perfection is not obligatory, and it is universally acknowledged that the concept of perfection is an unattainable ideal.

Avoid attempting to appear extroverted - Instead, strive to collaborate with individuals who do not cause you to feel overwhelmed or overstimulated. Acknowledge your proclivity to engage in lengthier cognitive deliberation compared to the majority of individuals.

Exercise caution in determining when it is appropriate to rely on your inherent inclination as opposed to when it is necessary to override it, such as discerning the most opportune moment to arrive at a resolution regarding a matter that has occupied your contemplation for a significant duration. (Boyes, 2013)

Cease engaging in self-deprecating dialogue - refrain from perceiving oneself through the lens of external judgment. Develop mindfulness whenever you engage in the act of juxtaposing yourself with others, and cease this behavior.

Cultivate a constructive mindset through the power of optimistic thoughts. Acknowledge the favorable attributes you possess, enhance their development, and attain additional ones.

Please ascertain and address any unfavorable attributes you might possess, such as engaging in self-deprecating talk, in order to eradicate them. Initially, it may prove to be challenging; hence, it is imperative to develop the ability to assume authority over the circumstances and refrain from succumbing to discouraging thoughts.

Please compose a comprehensive compilation of your favorable abilities and attributes. Reinforce your knowledge of these skills by periodically revisiting the aforementioned list.

Engage in daily positive self-affirmation on a consistent basis. Eliminate and disregard any detrimental internal dialogue that you may notice yourself engaging in.

Consider this: Introverted individuals possess a greater number of occasions to cultivate a robust sense of self-worth when compared to their extroverted counterparts.

Introverted individuals derive their cognitive vitality from introspection, solitude, and engaging in profound musings and reflections upon their thoughts and concepts. On the contrary, individuals with extroverted traits are motivated by external stimuli, finding energy and fulfillment through interpersonal connections.

That being said, extroverts are dependent on other people for their mental energy, while introverts only depend on themselves. The latter individuals also possess a propensity for engaging in introspection and self-examination, thereby deepening their understanding of themselves and cultivating personal growth.

Fundamentally, the more thorough your self-awareness, the greater your capacity for self-improvement and the cultivation of self-confidence will be.

There is a multitude of individuals who exhibit extroverted qualities and possess strong aptitude in social networking, which they skillfully leverage to their benefit. In the present-day society, it holds paramount significance to establish connections with individuals who are engaged in the study or professional occupation within your respective domain.

Introverts are extremely self-aware. In the presence of familiar acquaintances, they exhibit greater sociability, thoughtfulness, and affability.

In contrast, some individuals who are inclined towards extroversion engage in unproductive activities such as idle chatter, rather than utilizing the occasion to cultivate relationships that could potentially facilitate personal growth. Although extroverts may possess strong social and interpersonal capabilities, it is crucial to note that their possession of these skills does not guarantee a monopoly on confidence.

Self-assurance versus Self-assuredness – On occasion, introverted individuals may experience uncertainly distinguishing between self-confidence and self-esteem.

Self-assurance pertains to the perceptions and beliefs one holds regarding their capabilities. These sentiments may vary depending on the circumstances. As an illustration, it is possible for an individual to possess a robust sense of self-worth while simultaneously encountering diminished levels of confidence in their mathematical and scientific aptitude within an educational environment. Having a strong sense of self-love promotes the development of self-esteem, which subsequently enhances one's confidence.

An individual known to you might express sentiments of inadequacy and exhibit diminished self-esteem. It is plausible that they may have held stagnant career positions or faced demeaning treatment from their superiors. Likewise, they may have encountered toxic personal relationships that culminated in unfortunate outcomes. They frequently express sentiments such as "I have no value."

Recognizing the unfavorable nature of this script marks the initial stride towards transforming one's mindset.

Regarding self-confidence, these individuals exhibit admirable qualities as compassionate friends, actively involved in philanthropic work at animal shelters, demonstrating their commitment by adopting pets and patrolling the locality to rescue abandoned or injured animals. It is possible that they have forwarded their application to pursue education at a prestigious veterinary institution, with the aim of obtaining their degree and endeavoring towards establishing an additional animal shelter for the purpose of rescuing and providing medical care to a greater number of animals. They possess conviction in their objectives and are committed to exerting diligent effort to attain them.

Currently, this individual is directing their attention towards areas in which they possess a strong sense of confidence and actively striving to transform their patterns of negative self-dialogue. They are making an earnest effort to enhance their self-esteem and self-confidence. (Ahmed, 2017)

Cultivating an optimistic mindset and immersing oneself in a conducive environment, surrounded by individuals who provide unwavering support and encouragement towards accomplishing one's personal objectives, will significantly enhance both self-assurance and self-assurance.

Maintaining One's Self-Esteem in a Society that Embraces Extroversion

Introverts do have self-esteem. They are merely less inclined to derive their self-esteem from social interaction. They are more inclined to derive their self-worth internally. Nevertheless, this statement might not hold true for all introverted individuals. (Gaut, 2016)

There exist individuals who derive satisfaction from the knowledge that there exists no recorded visual evidence of them in an inebriated state partaking in foolish behaviors; moreover, they also possess a sense of self-esteem in maintaining a limited circle of confidants as opposed to a large network of casual acquaintances.

Introverts typically exhibit contentment with remaining in the periphery and exhibit limited inclination towards acquiring people's approval. Nonetheless, individuals who possess a creative inclination take great pride in garnering recognition for their innovative endeavors. This is due to the fact that the artwork possesses a self-expressive quality, obviating the necessity for verbal explanation from the artist.

In contrast, extroverts have a strong desire for societal validation. They desire to be popular and exhibit noticeable distress if someone holds unfavorable opinions about them. The manner in which they showcase and establish a connection with their personality is through their work, and they aspire for their achievements to gain recognition.

Extroverted individuals typically strive to cultivate an extensive social network, often deriving satisfaction from being affable towards diverse individuals or holding the esteem of colleagues within an establishment. The image they project serves as the bedrock of their self-worth and the manner in which they are acknowledged.

Both personalities are equally valid. Numerous individuals of introverted disposition take great pride in their ability to remain self-assured without seeking excessive validation from external influences, and possess a strong sense of authenticity. Extroverts take satisfaction in their ability to direct their attention towards themselves, thereby preventing the development of meaningful connections with others, and can effortlessly conform to the expectations of society.

4.3 Forgiveness

Assuming the role of a victim is a regrettable inclination that all individuals have succumbed to at some juncture in their lives. In order to comprehensively comprehend the reasoning behind your thoughts, it is necessary to alter the rhythm at which you engage and reflect. By acquiring a sense of mastery, one can effectively regulate these states and gain comprehension of them. Believing oneself to be a victim is not always unjustified; indeed, there are instances in which we are indisputably subject to victimization. From one perspective, each and every one of us is subject to the influences and circumstances of the world we inhabit. We are born into a societal framework characterized by stringent norms and obligations. The majority of families exert influence on children to conform to a specific lifestyle. In contemporary American society, there is a prevailing societal norm whereby individuals are expected to complete their college education and establish a family. This singular aspect does not constitute a significant misdirection; however, when compounded by additional expectations such as those pertaining to religious or financial matters, this can engender unwarranted pressure on individuals. They do fall prey to the system.

Can you ascertain additional instances where individuals are legitimately subjected to victimization due to the systemic apparatus? There are many examples. Racism exemplifies a situation wherein individuals become subjected to victimization by the societal framework, leaving them with no alternative but to confront their condition as victims. The heightened incarceration rates of individuals belonging to ethnic minorities, the geographical concentration of minority groups, and the existence of legal frameworks that disproportionately target and impact people of color and other marginalized communities can be attributed to systemic racism in the United States. The ratio will vary on an individual basis depending on the extent of bigotry's impact on their lives. Nevertheless, this serves as a prominent illustration of the prevailing state of victimhood among humanity; namely, that certain individuals have already endured victimization.

An alternative category encompasses individuals belonging to the working class or those who may be considered economically disadvantaged. This particular social group encounters structural barriers that impede their inclusion in certain income sectors of society, consequently limiting their accessibility to goods and services to a significantly lesser extent compared to individuals who belong to the middle or upper classes. This serves as an additional illustration of the necessity for certain individuals to confront the influences of societal constructs that have shaped the circumstances of their existence.

There is hope, however. Regardless of one's circumstances or the hardships they face, there must always exist an avenue for individuals to discover enlightenment. Uncovering sources of guidance and rekindling one's inner resolve remains an inherent facet of human nature. To effectively navigate the burdensome impositions established by societal norms and expectations, one must grant oneself the liberty to define their own path towards personal growth and resilience.

What steps do you plan to take in order to accomplish this? One may commence by recognizing the prevailing elements that subject one to oppression. I am cognizant of the systemic oppression I have endured throughout my upbringing due to socio-economic disadvantage, yet I am determined to employ my personal agency to alter my circumstances. An individual adopting a victim mentality would express, "I have encountered a series of unjust circumstances in the world, which is truly unfavorable." "I hereby tender my resignation." Although it is acknowledged that the initial assertion, "the world is unjust," holds truth, the subsequent portion of the statement does not align with reality.

The subject matter under discussion pertains to an inequitable global landscape. The global landscape is characterized by its unpredictable and unforgiving nature, as exemplified by the expansive tracts of wilderness that remains untouched by human presence. No discernible structure is present in these locations, save for the inherent natural order of the earth. Entropy is prevalent in these locations, namely the rainforests, swamps, deep deserts, and vast oceans with their enigmatic vastness. These locations exemplify the formidable challenges that life faces as a result of the world's harsh conditions. It is imperative to possess the capability to safeguard oneself physically against the perils that exist in the world in order to survive. One cannot sustain their existence without engendering their own sphere of existence. While it is within your prerogative to pursue that course of action, it undoubtedly presents certain challenges. In the natural world, there exists no intervening force, no human presence to observe the administration of justice. Individuals who possess diminished physical strength, those in the early stages of life, and those who have advanced in years frequently succumb to mortality.

Nevertheless, a profound dichotomy exists among individuals that compels us to strive for excellence, uphold justice, and exhibit moral conduct. This observation prompts us to discern the distinction between moral principles, and furthermore, it is evident that a considerable amount of malevolence permeates our society. Hence, it is imperative to comprehend that although humans possess the capability and inherent inclination toward benevolence, there exist numerous individuals who stumble and exhibit malevolent behavior. We cannot place complete and profound trust in the entirety of the human race. It is essential for us to exercise prudence in our trust, and prioritize our own well-being.

It is essential to develop a propensity for self-preservation without assuming the role of a victim. An individual who has been victimized lacks the capacity to advocate for their own interests as they are incapable of returning to a functional state. They are victimized, taken down by their own accord, and they have given up in the world.

One good reason not to play the victim is that it is not a fun role to play. The situation lacks a substantial narrative trajectory. The individual in question serves as the target of a criminal act, subsequently assuming the role of a lamenting figure who portrays their plight as a helpless, impoverished victim throughout the remainder of the narrative. Playing that role may not be advantageous for you. In life, we tend to have preferences for the roles we assume, and if this particular role does not align with your personality, it would be advisable to refrain from portraying yourself as the victim.

The individual lacks a true sense of identity. Numerous individuals experience traumatic events, through which they undergo personal growth, acquire knowledge, and evolve as a result. Individuals have the capacity to effectively manage and assimilate traumatic events and incorporate diverse life experiences into their overarching psyche. They allowed their traumatic experiences to fade into the past, embracing a sense of tranquility and refraining from dwelling on their past traumas except when necessary for the purpose of grieving appropriately.

Nevertheless, certain individuals develop an emotional attachment to their sorrow. They cling to it with fervor, as if it were a tale they wish to perpetually embrace, ultimately assuming the role of their life's narrative. It is disheartening to witness, as it often arises from circumstances beyond the individual's control, leaving them with little alternative but to persist.

Nevertheless, as they navigate this difficult experience and strive to cope with the resulting trauma, they inevitably suffer impairments in specific aspects of their self-perception, yet fail to acquire the necessary knowledge or skills to rectify said impairments. These individuals are characterized by their propensity to constantly revisit their challenging experiences or trauma in their thoughts, unable to fully overcome their effects. They perceive themselves as individuals afflicted with cancer, victims of depression, or offspring of alcohol-dependent parents, thus adopting these circumstances as their defining characteristics.

This is the problem. It is not possible for a negative concept to serve as the foundation of your identity. The sole burden of carrying with you lies not solely in experiences such as being afflicted by cancer or facing mistreatment. Think about it. If that is the underlying belief that is persistently being reiterated, consider the implications of such a mindset on your self-perception. It indicates that you perpetually reside in proximity to mortality, or at least your psyche perceives a concern. This lifestyle is highly undesirable, and an individual must attain complete assimilation in order to achieve genuine advancement in their self-actualization. An individual who abstains from making efforts to overcome obstacles and advance in their life will be actively evading the discomfort associated with personal development. However, it is in this evasion that they unknowingly inflict significant suffering upon themselves in the future.

Enhancing Self-Esteem Enhances Decision-Making Confidence

One additional advantage associated with possessing a robust sense of self-worth is the capacity to enhance one's self-assurance in the process of making decisions. Because an individual's life is predominantly shaped by the choices they make, individuals lacking self-esteem significantly suffer from the distress caused by this veracity. When an individual possesses a sense of self-worth, they are capable of acknowledging their own desires and requirements. By acquiring knowledge of those elements, the act of making decisions becomes significantly more straightforward as one possesses a clear comprehension of their objective and is resolute in selecting a course of action that aligns with said objective. Individuals who possess minimal self-esteem tend to engage in prolonged introspection and meticulously envision every possible outcome of failure within their thoughts. They become embroiled in the anxiety stemming from concerns about societal opinions or judgments regarding their choice.

In order to provide you with a more comprehensive comprehension, the following are several ramifications that result from a dearth of confidence in the process of decision-making:

• Analysis Paralysis in the Process of Making Decisions

Individuals with diminished self-esteem have a tendency to refrain from making decisions due to feeling excessively daunted throughout the decision-making process. Frequently, individuals find themselves constrained in their current position due to their inclination to remain in their comfort zone instead of taking the risk of making an unfavorable choice.

- Absence of Trust in Decision-Making Processes

Individuals with diminished self-confidence encounter difficulties in harboring faith that the choice they have made proves advantageous. They will endeavor to persuade themselves that they ought to have taken an alternative course of action.

- Reluctance to Assume Responsibility

In circumstances necessitating significant decisions, individuals with diminished self-esteem may attempt to transfer the responsibility of making such decisions to someone else. In this manner, they can attain a sense of tranquility and maintain confidence in the capacity of another individual to arrive at a superior resolution. They perceive themselves to possess lower capability and intelligence, thereby justifying the decision-making role of others. In the event that circumstances deviate unfavorably as a result of this, individuals can readily attribute accountability to said person for their decision.

• Diminishing opportunities in life • Constricting range of possibilities • Decreasing avenues for advancement in life

Individuals who possess a diminished sense of self-worth may discover that their opportunities in life steadily diminish. They are considerably more prone to overlooking opportunities that could have potentially proven advantageous for them. For instance, an individual might hold the belief that their present occupation represents the pinnacle of their professional opportunities, or that their current role signifies the apex of their career trajectory, whereas others may perceive them as capable of attaining greater accomplishments. Due to their self-imposed restrictions, they encounter challenges in mustering the drive necessary to seek new opportunities or advancements.

In gaining an understanding of the repercussions associated with harboring inadequate self-assurance in the realm of decision-making, my aspiration is that this knowledge will serve as a catalyst for your motivation to enhance your self-confidence. Possessing the requisite level of self-assurance to decisively make choices will enhance an individual's ability to uncover abundant prospects in life and foster self-reliance in their decision-making abilities. The underlying principles of decision making are rooted in an individual's self-esteem, and thus, the initiation of self-love and self-respect serves as the initial stride towards progress. Individuals may discover that as they develop a deeper comprehension of their desires, requirements, and objectives, their ability to make decisions will gradually improve.

Goal Setting Obstacles

Numerous individuals hold the belief that goal setting is merely deceptive and lacks effectiveness. If one does not possess a thorough comprehension of the efficacy underlying adequate goal setting, it can prove challenging to allocate the necessary time from one's schedule to genuinely establish a goal.

To comprehend the significance of goal setting, it is recommended to peruse numerous literary works on success, wherein you will discover that the most accomplished individuals establish achievable objectives and diligently integrate them into their daily routines.

Even individuals who achieve rapid success have not truly accomplished everything within a short span of time. It entailed several evenings of diligently adhering to a meticulously devised strategy that yielded favorable outcomes.

You appear to be uncertain regarding the method to establish an attainable objective.

If you have previously attempted to establish objectives but encountered inadequate outcomes, it is likely due to a lack of proficiency in goal-setting. It is not as straightforward as merely documenting a reverie. Goals aren't dreams.

These are practical, precise, attainable outcomes that you desire to observe. Devote sufficient time to acquiring knowledge about the most effective techniques for goal setting, enabling the attainment of success in setting goals.

You possess a fear of unsuccessful outcomes.

Numerous individuals refrain from establishing objectives due to harboring a self-imposed conviction that they are destined for failure regardless. Consequently, in the absence of establishing an objective, they will be able to avoid experiencing defeat.

It is important to bear in mind that prioritizing success in planning, rather than planning for failure, is a practical approach. Setting goals is not only a recipe for failure but rather, it is an assured recipe for success. Once you acknowledge that genuine success can solely be attained through the establishment of objectives, you will triumph over this hindrance.

You have a fear of being subjected to criticism or evaluation.
At times, individuals experience apprehension when it comes to establishing objectives for certain matters due to perceiving them as excessive. For example, consider the scenario where you aspire to pursue a Master's degree by returning to college, or alternatively, if you have the desire to establish your own business venture.
You harbor apprehensions that the public disclosure of your intended objective may subject you to severe scrutiny or reproach, primarily due to a perceived moral or conjectured concern.
If you are concerned regarding the perceptions of others about yourself, it is indubitably a suitable moment to delve into the inner most realms of your being and transcend such trepidations. The

veracity is, your perception of yourself holds greater significance than any other factor. Once you cease assessing yourself, you will no longer be concerned with the evaluation of others.

You are apprehensive of achieving success.

Surprisingly, there are individuals who harbor a genuine fear of achieving success. They experience excessive levels of stress and expectations related to achieving success, which hinders their ability to set and attain goals for success. They derive greater comfort from assuming a role of mediocrity or being perceived as "average" rather than as individuals who set objectives, strive to attain them, and are recognized as successful.

It is a fact that there will perpetually exist individuals who desire to dismantle your accomplishments when you attain success. However, the most sorrowful aspect of life is the feeling of remorse caused by the failure to engage in certain endeavors. The majority of individuals often lament the actions they failed to undertake, rather than the actions they did undertake, regardless of their moral implications.

You harbor private doubts about your self-worth.

The importance lies in one's perception of oneself, for if one views oneself as lacking follow-through, lacking success, and lacking the ability to transform one's life, one will actively avoid engaging in the process of goal setting.

You possess exclusive agency over your actions, rendering you solely responsible for establishing goals and generating a sense of self-worth.

Do you hold a different perspective regarding the feasibility of this?

Individuals tend to refrain from engaging in goal setting due to their inability to envision the potential outcomes and possibilities that can be attained. They don't believe. They do not envision themselves completely attaining success, nor do they genuinely experience success. Due to their perception of its impossibility, they fail to make an effort.

However, the reality is that you cannot ascertain with certainty about any matter unless you diligently pursue the requisite measures to achieve an objective. You have the ability to envision ambitious goals and strive for extraordinary achievements. In many spheres, the act of exerting effort holds greater significance than achieving success itself. Furthermore, it is highly probable that with sincere effort, you will ultimately succeed.

Combining The Strategies

It has come to our attention that at some point, you began to harbor a sense of disapproval towards your own identity as a member of the human race. The specific factors leading to this occurrence, such as critical evaluation, dismissal, or the influence of parents or peers, remain undisclosed. It has been established that the impact of such an emotion is consistent in nature, as it poses constraints on one's self-esteem. Put simply, you harbor uncertainties regarding your own abilities and consequently experience a dearth of confidence.

We provided you with a detailed discussion on different strategies, and upon initial assessment, we have compiled the following recommendations to help you overcome your lack of confidence:

Develop an awareness of your negative triggers – Put simply, foster a comprehensive comprehension of the origins of this influx of negativity. This enables you to effectively disregard the negative aspects and focus on the positive elements in order to overcome them. The greater the disapproval or negative feedback you have encountered, the more imperative it is for you to focus on cultivating self-acceptance. The opinions of others hold no significance in relation to one's identity. They are not obligated to lead your existence. You do. It is imperative that you acknowledge adverse influences and distance yourself from their presence. Upon identifying these triggers or individuals that evoke negative feelings, one can take proactive measures to minimize their interaction with such stimuli. In the event that these occurrences are limited to your cognitive processes, we have also provided guidance on employing mindfulness techniques to disengage from such thoughts.

Negative triggers may arise from contemplation of individuals who have abandoned or betrayed you, or the apprehension of spending time with individuals who elicit discomfort and self-doubt. Consider your circle of acquaintances and analyze which individuals uplift your spirits when in their presence, and which ones tend to elicit concerns and negative feelings about your own self. What situations trigger insecurity? It is essential that you acknowledge them, as without doing so, you will be unable to rectify the situation or prevent potential triggers. Prior to developing a robust sense of self-worth, it is crucial to establish an effective means of circumventing the influences exacerbating the descent into pessimism.

Cultivating self-care and nurturing your self-worth – The subsequent strategy revolved around practicing self-compassion and allocating time towards meaningful endeavors like volunteer work, as these activities contribute to the development of your self-assurance and foster a positive self-perception." These matters did not require the validation of others. These endeavors were directed towards enhancing the quality of your life and fostering a constructive self-perception. This is so important. You possess equal worth to every individual on this planet; however, when you persist in diminishing your true potential, it undermines your self-assurance.

Embracing one's own existence - The approach focused on self-love entails nurturing one's identity and prioritizing the pursuit of activities that bring joy and fulfillment. It is of utmost significance that you engage in and upon discovering leisure activities that captivate your genuine interest, you might even come across individuals who share similar preferences. Nevertheless, by prioritizing these aspirations of yours, you will gain a genuine understanding of your aptitude in the domains that bring you enjoyment. If you are aware of having available time, dedicate it to engaging in constructive endeavors of which you possess a strong affinity. It is ultimately your responsibility to enhance the quality of your life, ensuring that upon waking each morning, you experience a sense of satisfaction and self-appreciation. If you are unable to accomplish that, it is beyond the capability of anyone else to do it on your behalf.

Respiration and Mindfulness – By integrating this type of practice into your daily routine, it fosters a sense of belonging and assists in achieving equilibrium in one's perception of the physical self and the environment. It is recommended that you make a daily attempt at this. Allocating just thirty minutes per day to the practice of mindfulness can greatly contribute to the development of self-assurance. Furthermore, it is possible to engage in physical activities throughout the day when experiencing strong negativity or apprehension towards unfamiliar tasks.

One illustration of this is employing breathing techniques prior to a meeting, which facilitates the process of quieting the mind, enabling enhanced mental acuity and allowing for greater contribution during the meeting. That's important.

From the instant you arise in the morning to the instant you retire in the evening, it is imperative that these strategies become an integral component of your daily existence. Know who you are. Embrace your true self and refrain from subjecting yourself to the expectations imposed by others. Alternatively, should you fail to adequately address this concern, you may find yourself falling short, resulting in a diminished sense of self-assurance.

Mindfulness can serve as a means to eliminate detrimental thoughts from one's mind. Rather than succumbing to thoughts of incapability and evading a task, alter your perspective to focus on the present moment and observe your surroundings. Find inspiration in the weather. Embrace the chance to excel and take solace in taking deep breaths until you regain composure to make another attempt. Indeed, there may exist certain limitations in life; however, it is imperative to persist and derive satisfaction from the awareness of one's innate adaptability, for it is often greater than perceived. Avoid convincing yourself that you are incapable of achieving something. Convince yourself that every instant in your existence presents a fresh prospect to engage in novel endeavors and determine their suitability for incorporation into your life.

The Collaboration Between Happiness And Self-Recognition Is Mutually Influential.

According to Robert Holden in his literary work titled Happiness Now!, it is observed that joy and self-recognition are interconnected. Truly, the level of self-awareness you possess determines the level of happiness you experience. The higher level of self-awareness you possess, the greater satisfaction you will enable yourself to recognize, attain, and savor. Given these circumstances, you experience a level of happiness proportional to what you willingly embrace, thus asserting your deservingness of it."

First and foremost, the cultivation of self-awareness mandates the cultivation of self-empathy. We can strengthen our relationship with ourselves only when we are capable of fully understanding and absolving ourselves of the things that we previously believed to be our own fault.

In order to adopt a more appreciative stance that serves our own interests – a fundamental indicator of self-acceptance – it is crucial to recognize that hitherto, we have merely felt compelled to demonstrate our worth to others, much like we initially believed we had to comply with the critical authority of our parents. Our support for these practices, regardless of their accuracy, has been a reflection of the legacy of our parents' unwavering affection.

Conducting a genuine inquiry into what I would consider to be our nearly pervasive state undoubtedly fosters a heightened sense of self-empathy. It is inherently compassionate that we can ascertain the means to enhance our self-love and perceive ourselves as deserving of admiration and esteem due to our sincere determination to confront and overcome the aspects of ourselves that we have struggled to accept.

One could argue that each and every one of us bears "emotional wounds resulting from experiences of conditional love" in our distant past. We find ourselves in the midst of those who are physically impaired yet mobile. Furthermore, this recognition of our shared human condition can serve as a catalyst for cultivating consistent acts of benevolence and selflessness, not only for our own benefit but also for the well-being of others.

In order to cultivate a greater sense of self-acceptance, we ought to commence by regularly and, ideally, with growing assurance, acknowledging that given the predominance of our biased self-referential convictions, we have exerted our utmost effort. In light of the circumstances, it is imperative for us to reevaluate any persistent notions of fault, as well as our myriad internal responses and derogatory statements. We must strive to confront and acknowledge the aspects of ourselves that we tend to ignore, and as individuals responsible for our own healing, extend empathy and understanding to every instance of self-rejection or denial. Therefore, we can begin to dismantle distorted emotions of culpability and shame, relying on measurements that simply failed to accurately depict what could reasonably be expected of us during that period.

The widely recognized French expression, 'Tout comprendre, c'est tout excuser' (literally, 'to understand all is to pardon all') constitutes a principle that should be applied universally, both towards ourselves and towards others, in any given situation. Through such actions, we can ascertain the precise reasons for our previous commitment to a singular objective and subsequently absolve ourselves of this behavior while ensuring its non-recurrence in the future.

To develop greater self-acceptance, it is imperative that we acknowledge the fact that we are not excessively responsible for any single matter, be it our articulation, comprehension, or any other imperfect behaviors we may exhibit. Our actions have been limited by a combination of fundamental principles and scientific knowledge. Moving forward, we unequivocally have the capacity and generally consider taking responsibility for actions in which we have caused harm or mistreated others. In any event, if our objective is to effectively cultivate self-acceptance, it is imperative that we approach this task with compassion and forgiveness imbued within our beings. We must acknowledge the specific circumstances, taking into consideration our internal conditioning up until that moment; our capacity for alternate action was extremely limited.

"Self-Pardon"

In order to attain personal liberation and nurture a state of boundless self-validation, it is imperative that we cultivate a mindset of "self-forgiveness" for our missteps, irrespective of their veracity. Ultimately, it may be comprehended that there is no need for forgiveness. Despite deviating from our previous determinations, it could be argued that we consistently acted blamelessly - endeavoring to the best of our abilities, considering (1) inherent traits or predispositions, (2) the persuasiveness of our desires and emotions, and (3) societal norms that we embraced at that particular period.

The determinant of perilous conduct, ultimately, is linked to common psychological safeguards. Furthermore, it borders on unrelenting for us to indict ourselves or view ourselves with contempt for engaging in behaviors that, in the moment, we believed necessary to protect ourselves from anxiety, shame, or emotional distress in general.

Nevertheless, it signifies a fundamental aspect of our predisposition and must be effectively integrated if we are to fully develop. As long as the fragmented aspects of ourselves are not acknowledged or embraced, achieving a complete and comprehensive self-awareness will continue to elude us indefinitely.

Once we are adequately prepared to discern the origin of these dull, unresponsive aspects within ourselves, any self-evaluation associated with them becomes not only severe but also disgraceful. Indeed, it is a fact that virtually everyone harbors prohibited (and, at times, nonsensical) desires and aspirations - irrespective of whether they entail causing harm to an individual who offends us, exerting unwarranted dominance over others, or even engaging in public nudity on a regular basis. Once we are prepared to acknowledge this, we are furthermore considerably advanced in embracing ourselves unconditionally. Recognizing that, notwithstanding their atypical or regrettable nature, the overwhelming majority of our "destructive fantasies" likely involve minimal contemplation of insults, damages, or hardships we have previously faced, we are now able to reinterpret these "variations" as, in fact, quite ordinary.

Furthermore, as we begin to recognize and accept our darker aspects, we can maintain deliberate control over the manner in which these aspects are expressed, ensuring the well-being of both ourselves and others. We will invariably approach every situation with love and nurturing, given the ability to reconnect with our innermost authentic essence. Hence, it is beyond our capacity to engage in any actions that would undermine our inherent proclivity for compassion and identification with the entirety of humanity. Possessing and integrating our various facets constitutes an exceptional experience. Furthermore, when we, or rather, our perceptions of ourselves, no longer experience a sense of isolation from others, any reprehensible justification for causing them harm dissipates.

It should be evident at this point that self-recognition bears no relevance to engaging in self-enhancement in that regard. As it does not pertain to remedying or rectifying anything within ourselves. By engaging in self-acknowledgment, we are effectively verifying and acknowledging our true identity, devoid of any biased evaluations, encompassing both our positive attributes and areas for improvement that exist in the present moment.

One drawback of centering one's focus on personal growth is that it inherently limits the ability to recognize oneself. Additionally, it is crucial to note that our ability to feel safe and content hinges on constantly striving for self-improvement. Self-recognition is contingent upon the present circumstances, rather than being contingent on future arrangements, as in the statement: "I will be fine when ." . After attaining the desired outcome. . . I will be fine." Self-assurance entails being in a stable state, devoid of any limitations or uncertainties. We do not necessarily disregard or reject our shortcomings or weaknesses; rather, we perceive them as being inconsequential compared to our essential worthiness.

Finally, it is solely our own efforts and actions that serve as the standard for recognizing our own worth. In addition, when we opt to discontinue self-assessment or self-monitoring, we can adopt a mindset of non-judgmental forgiveness. In fact, if we refrain from our ingrained inclination to self-study and critically examine ourselves, and instead strive to understand our past actions with empathy, we will come to realize that there is truly nothing to apologize for (as the saying goes, "Tout comprendre..."). Affirmatively, we can assure that there will be advancements in the future, however, we must also objectively recognize our current state, without disregarding our imperfections.

And in this context, I cannot adequately argue that it is feasible to recognize and value ourselves while remaining dedicated to a lifelong pursuit of self-improvement. Embracing ourselves as we are does not imply that we will lack the motivation to make improvements or advancements that will make us more effective or positively impact our own lives and the lives of others. The fundamental notion lies in the fact that self-acknowledgment remains detached from these changes in every aspect. It is not imperative for us to diligently ensure our self-acknowledgment; it suffices to alter our perception of ourselves. Therefore, it appears that altering our practices is solely a question of personal preference, rather than being crucial for enhancing one's self-esteem on a larger scale.

It pertains to originating from a markedly distinct location. If self-acknowledgment is to be "attained," a result of exerting discipline upon ourselves, then it imposes limitations - constantly at risk. The perpetual process of embracing oneself can never be concluded. Attaining a perfect grade in any pursuit through which we evaluate ourselves can only provide us with a transient respite from our continuous efforts. The understanding that we instill in ourselves is that our worth is determined solely by our most recent achievement. It is seemingly unattainable to achieve a state of self-recognition due to unintentionally perceiving our pursuit of such recognition as perpetually enduring.

By adhering to such exacting standards, we inadvertently endorse the methods employed by our own loving parents. Nevertheless, we are undoubtedly failing to acknowledge our own worth or to treat ourselves with the consideration and mindfulness that our parents failed to provide for us.

In conclusion, it is only when we reach a state of complete self-affirmation - by cultivating an enhanced sense of self-compassion and focusing predominantly on our strengths rather than weaknesses - that we can ultimately absolve ourselves of our shortcomings and relinquish our dependence on external validation. We have undoubtedly made mistakes. However, this holds true for every individual, without exception. The essence of our character does not truly align with our error (as such an association would suggest an unfortunate occurrence of "misidentification"!)

Finally, there is no justification for refraining from contemporaneously electing to overhaul the fundamental sentiment encompassing our sense of self. Additionally, it is essential to bear in mind that our respective imperfections contribute to our inherent humanity. Should all of our imperfections and shortcomings abruptly cease to exist, it is my conjecture that we would instantaneously undergo a metamorphosis into luminous white light and subsequently become nonexistent in this earthly realm. By doing so, while striving for authentic self-acceptance, we might even have to cultivate a sense of discrete satisfaction in our imperfections. Taking into account all factors, if we were without any flaws whatsoever, we would never have the opportunity to undertake this profoundly challenging ordeal.

External Validation

I arrived at my workplace that morning in the usual manner, as I do every day. I felt ok. I had a meeting with my manager, wherein I was commended for my efforts and achievements in my work. I experienced a sense of excitement and satisfaction in myself. I experienced a sense of significance and believed that my efforts were making a valuable contribution to the workplace.

I perceived myself as having inherent worth... Excellent work, Jonny!

Subsequently, towards the end of the day, while engaged in administrative tasks, I attended to my e-mail and came across a correspondence from a different manager whom I had previously served under. I accessed my email inbox with the purpose of reviewing the progress of a task I had completed.

Jon, it required a significant amount of time on my part to complete this editing task. Please give the content your undivided attention, as I believe it is of utmost importance.

Your performance in your role, Jonny, is notably inadequate. You're useless. I was internally chastising myself, expressing that I was incapable of executing any task accurately.

The direction of my state was entirely influenced by the external sources that I had acquired. I did not exert personal agency and self-regulation in shaping my self-perception. Undoubtedly, it is commonplace for individuals to experience fluctuations in their emotions, yet I remained consistently attentive in this manner. I'm not alone.

Now, let us consider an instance involving my acquaintance, Bill. Incidentally, I must clarify that I do not possess an acquaintance by the name of Bill, and the narrative under discussion is one that I have reconstructed. Bill was in a romantic relationship with a young lady for whom he held deep affection.

Upon receiving communication from her, he was exhilarated and elated, experiencing a profound sense of joy and satisfaction.

However, in instances when Bill did not receive any communication from her, he would inevitably entertain the most pessimistic thoughts. He experienced a profound sense of insignificance and despair, as he believed no one held any regard for him. He would never garner the interest or attraction of young women.

Can you perceive the predicament involving these two individuals (one of whom is myself)? Their self-perception is heavily influenced by external factors. If an endeavor yields favorable outcomes, it instills a sense of self-satisfaction within them. If it does not, then they do not. This phenomenon is perilous, yet lamentably prevalent.

Indeed, let us assign it a designation, notwithstanding the likelihood that it may already possess one. How about: somethingelse-itis?

"You express immense creativity, Jonny," you remark. Awww, thanks.

In order to overcome the condition known as somethingelse-itis, it is imperative that we enhance our self-esteem. By doing so, we can cultivate a steadfast sense of self-acceptance, regardless of the outcomes we face, even in challenging circumstances.

"Let us put an end to the fictional narratives of:

I am deficient in my personal worthiness in the absence of a romantic partner.

I cannot consider myself successful until I attain the desired number of followers.

I do not consider myself proficient unless I attain such a significant sum of money.

We do not possess direct authority over those matters. What factors do we have influence over, consequently? Our endeavors to advance in these matters. Learn to love what you do and value what you do.

This is within your purview of influence. Learn to praise yourself. And similar to any other aptitude, cultivating self-appreciation can be acquired through intentional practice.

Adverse outcomes and refusals may pose challenges, therefore, kindly refrain from hastily assuming a pessimistic attitude of resignation, such as thinking, "Oh well, I did my best."

You may continue to experience disappointments; however, by cultivating a stronger sense of self-appreciation and acknowledging your own efforts, you can effectively mitigate the impact on your self-esteem.

Here is one inquiry that you could pose, which I have posed:

I am inquisitive about the potential outcomes should I embark on an endeavor, and yet ultimately encounter failure.

We should consider adopting a novel strategy. Seeking guidance from a mentor, coach, or experienced individual can prove immensely beneficial in this regard. In the absence of an alternative approach, there is a likelihood of succumbing to a state of insanity by incessantly engaging in repetitive actions without yielding desired outcomes.

Action

Limiting the duration of phone usage and minimizing engagement with social media platforms is conducive to abstaining from seeking external validation. How can one feasibly derive a sense of self-contentment when the external world incessantly imposes societal judgments and expectations regarding one's appearance, behavior, and so forth? As an aspiring author, I am consistently provided guidance on the optimal approach to promote my book, procure numerous presentation opportunities, and effectively market my coaching enterprise.

It is not advisable to abruptly cut off all contact, as this could potentially result in even more frequent checking of messages and social media platforms in search of validation.

Contrarily, allocate specific periods during which you can abstain from using your phone in order to concentrate on self-reflection, as well as designate intervals in which you partake in serene strolls.

A leisurely stroll unaccompanied by music, solely dedicated to introspection and devoid of technological distractions, aimed at cultivating heightened mindfulness and connection with one's immediate environment. Creating an environment of mental spaciousness greatly benefits cognitive functioning. Even the presence of podcasts and music has the potential to disrupt this mental environment and incite various trains of thought.

Strategies for cultivating presence:

● Contemplation. There exists a plethora of applications and methodologies worth contemplating. I would suggest allocating a duration of fifteen minutes for engaging in nasal inhalation and exhalation.

● Allocating brief periods throughout the day to engage in mindful observation of one's surroundings.

● Engaging in daily journaling for a duration of ten minutes to document and reflect upon one's thoughts and emotions.

The Actions Of Others Serve As An Indication Of Their Character, Rather Than A Reflection Of Your Own.

At the age of sixteen, I secured my initial employment as a part-time shop assistant operating the cash registers at Somerfield, presently known as Co-Op. Initially, I held a rather unfavorable view of it, but I found myself compelled to undertake the task. In fact, I jammily got the job when they employed me for working Saturdays, but they misunderstood and then I told them I couldn't do Saturdays. During that time, my level of self-assurance was not particularly high. However, the significance of participating in Saturday football with my father was such that I could not bear to abstain from it. Therefore, I commenced my employment on Monday evenings.

At that juncture of my life, I did not possess a fervor for personal growth or similar pursuits; instead, my passion was primarily directed towards football. I had a moderate level of skill in the activity, however, I greatly enjoyed observing Yeovil engage in matches throughout various regions of the country.

During that period, I was primarily focused on my education and attempting to assimilate amongst my peers. This endeavor involved acquiring extravagant accessories such as an ostentatious gold chain, as well as experimenting with unconventional grooming choices like a sculpted eyebrow, intricately styled hair, and even a completely shaved head at one juncture. Whatever was I thinking?

Nevertheless, diverging from the narrative. I was employed in Crewkerne,

Somerset, a small town which, to be frank, did not captivate my interest, although it presently boasts a splendid branch of Waitrose. Crewkerne was home to individuals who exhibited both amiability and less-than-desirable attitudes.

Upon reaching the age of eighteen, it became within my purview to exercise my consent or refusal of requests for alcoholic beverages. Occasionally, it is observed that when a shop assistant vocalizes a request for consent, a customer might respond by uttering the phrase 'yes please'... Quite amusing indeed. (Emphasizing a facetious tone)

On a certain occasion, my junior colleague conveyed this statement, prompting me to politely request identification from a young lady who appeared to be in the age range of 17 to 20. I was greeted with the remark, "You imbecilic ignoramus! I appear sufficiently mature." Could it be argued that the expression "You derogatory term!" is indicative of my own character? Did I behave foolishly?

I would prefer if your response to that question were to be in the negative, therefore let us continue with a negative response.

In my younger years, I experienced a pervasive sense of personal inadequacy. Indeed, the young woman was merely experiencing discontent or distress with herself and contemplating upon it. It did not bear any resemblance to my character.

The incident, nonetheless, had a detrimental impact on my self-confidence. It is crucial to prioritize assisting a wide range of individuals in cultivating elevated self-esteem, as individuals who have been wounded tend to project their pain onto others. Individuals who possess a strong sense of self-worth do not engage in deliberate acts of harm towards others in such a manner.

There was no evidence to support the claim that my behavior was inappropriate in this particular situation. Nevertheless, the brain, being the mastermind, remains vigilant for potential threats. It identifies and prioritizes negative aspects by placing greater emphasis on emotions rather than objective facts when presented with such instances.

I have an additional anecdote to share in relation to this matter.

Zack, whom I presented as my partner, was involved in a romantic relationship.

Congratulations, Zack my friend; that is fantastic. An inadvertent rhyme is occurring…

Regardless, on a certain day, Zack returned to his abode only to stumble upon his girlfriend engaging in a passionate embrace with another gentleman. Zack was filled with sorrow and began weeping profusely. Subsequently, he endured months of fragmentation. This was comprehensible, considering the recent events he had experienced. Zack needed time to get over this, but he also had the belief it was his fault. Can it be attributed to Zack? Currently, it is conceivable that Zack may have exhibited negative behavior such as being an inadequate partner or displaying negligence towards her, although it is important to clarify that he did not engage in such behavior. However, the indisputably destructive action in question is undeniably the act of infidelity.

By what means did Zack manage to exercise control or deter the illicit behavior of another individual?

The actions of others do not in any way define you; individuals are solely accountable for their own aberrant behavior. One can solely endeavor to exert maximum effort, exert influence upon others, and provide assistance to them. One cannot alter the nature of an individual; rather, an individual is solely responsible for facilitating their own transformation or self-improvement.

This is particularly bothersome to me when witnessing someone reconcile with their unfaithful partner as it essentially conveys the message that infidelity is permissible. What truly concerns me is the significant deficiency in self-esteem that an individual exhibits through such actions.

I indeed experienced a comparable scenario in my personal life, although it did not involve infidelity within a committed relationship. During my early twenties, I was involved in a romantic relationship which seemed promising. However, I acknowledge that I was excessively aloof in my approach, thus undermining my chances for successful dating experiences. I must admit that my skills in communicating via text messages are subpar. Subsequently, she expressed doubts regarding my level of interest in her, despite the fact that we indulged in intimate moments like kissing, going on dates, and her meeting someone else, which made her uncertain about choosing between me and the aforementioned individual.

At that moment, my reply consisted of expressing my fondness towards you and urging you to select me, albeit not verbatim. That demonstrates a significant level of disrespect towards me. I came to the realization that I had been convincing myself of the necessity of seeking validation from an individual who expressed uncertain sentiments towards me. That young woman possessed remarkable qualities and demonstrated exemplary character. Although we were not engaged in a formal relationship during the initial stages of our courtship, I regretfully mishandled my approach. Throughout the passing years, I have gained valuable insights and wisdom from this experience. She simply did not possess the emotional connection towards me, and while this is acceptable, it does not serve as a reflection of my character. I believed so during that period.

Action:

This is a potent technique that I personally engage in. I maintain a contemplative state of quietude, engaging in introspection to ponder upon my emotional state, acknowledging the thoughts that arise and endeavoring to comprehend their underlying nature. As an illustration, I inquire, "What are the factors contributing to the falsehood of this belief?" Additionally, I have appended a series of supplementary inquiries.

What emotions are currently evident within me?

What is the root cause of this situation?

What emotions am I seeking to experience? (Not the outcome)

- What aspects are within my sphere of influence?

- What is the intuition indicating?

Transformation Of Failure Into Triumph

The majority of individuals have a limited tolerance for significant letdowns in their lives, after which their excitement wanes and they revert their attention towards their diminished self-worth. Acquire the ability to direct your attention towards minor achievements. Transform those instances of defeat into minor triumphs, and in turn, transmute those minor triumphs into larger ones.

In the event of initial failure...

The correlation between success and self-esteem is highly significant. Immediate success enhances one's self-esteem in the present moment. Self-esteem breeds success. They became husband and wife, and together they navigate their journey through life, holding each other's hands. Thus, one must ponder whether the aforementioned axiom, which suggests persistent efforts in the face of initial failures, should be regarded as an indisputable fact or as the most valuable counsel for enhancing one's sense of self-worth.

Individuals who suffer from a lack of confidence might find it exceedingly formidable to envision themselves achieving success. For individuals with diminished self-confidence, perceiving success can prove to be a formidable task as they fail to acknowledge it when it presents itself, even at their doorstep.

For certain individuals, success is solely reliant on persevering, ensuring their ability to navigate through each passing day. For some individuals, it entails a genuine transition from harboring feelings of low self-regard to achieving a state of self-acceptance. That transition necessitates a thorough examination of the events occurring in your life and implementing modifications. Should you choose to refrain from making alterations and persisting with the identical course of action, your self-esteem shall suffer detriment without any opportunity for enhancement.

Nevertheless, if you are able to introspect and assess your behavior, language, and thought patterns, and subsequently implement even the slightest modifications, this will effectively enhance your self-esteem. As emphasized in the preceding chapter, one's self-esteem is significantly influenced by their thoughts, verbal expressions, and internal dialogues. All manifestations have the potential to materialize in the physical realm – you ultimately embody your thoughts.

When confronted with a failure, it is essential to introspect and scrutinize the reasons for the failure rather than merely perceiving oneself as a failure. By doing so, one should endeavor to identify the underlying causes of the failure and subsequently implement transformative adjustments within oneself, regardless of their magnitude, as a result. Do not fixate on the occurrence of failure; instead, endeavor to comprehend its underlying cause and implement necessary modifications. By engaging in this practice, one can transform failures into stepping stones to achieve success.

Adversity paves the way to achieving success. You shall acquire strength rather than diminishing it. You will enhance your self-esteem rather than experiencing its erosion through failure. We encounter failures with the intention of conducting analysis, implementing necessary revisions, and attempting anew. Pursuing the same course of action repeatedly while anticipating a different outcome, without making any alterations, cannot be deemed as a manifestation of success. Alternatively, it is referred to as being insane. Nevertheless, in the event of failure, it is vital to conduct a thorough analysis and implement necessary adjustments, as this will result in incremental accomplishments until ultimate success is achieved, thereby significantly enhancing one's self-confidence.

The 'Ah Ha' Moment

One highly captivating aspect to anticipate while striving towards enhancing one's self-esteem is the epiphany, colloquially known as the 'Ah Ha' moment. What precisely constitutes the 'Ah Ha' moment? It can be characterized as an occurrence of abrupt realization or significant revelation. It may manifest as an instance of profound lucidity wherein all elements align and become perceptible. The moment of epiphany, if acknowledged, can be a moment of exceptional lucidity that enhances one's sense of self-worth.

The phenomenon commonly referred to as the 'Ah Ha' moment is also recognized in certain circles as the eureka effect. It manifests throughout the spectrum of human experiences, wherein a previously incomprehensible concept is suddenly and instantaneously grasped. This particular moment serves as the catalyst for gaining valuable insights.

Gaining a thorough understanding of reality has the ability to propel one away from self-doubt and diminished self-regard, towards a state of assurance and resilience.

The "Ah Ha" moment can be characterized as a pivotal breakthrough. It serves as a space where individuals can overcome their diminished self-confidence and personal uncertainties. It frequently proves challenging for an individual to overcome the cognitive barriers posed by diminished self-regard. The occurrence of an epiphany is incredibly rapid, profoundly illuminating, and divinely aligned, shattering the barriers that confine you and transporting you to a realm beyond your familiar boundaries and self-perception. Allowing it to happen will result in a boost in one's self-esteem.

Summary and Action Plan

In this chapter, we embark upon a transformative journey towards heightened self-esteem and the implementation of strategies that facilitate the cultivation of increased self-worth. In this fourth step, we present a series of targeted exercises that can effectively enhance one's self-esteem.

• You are yourself. You possess a singular identity, hence I implore you to cease making such comparisons to others. Please document a comprehensive inventory of your talents, outlooks, and principles in life. Conduct a comparison between your emotional state yesterday and your present state of being. Note the difference.

• Exercise purposefulness. Prior to rising from your sleeping quarters in the early morning, establish your intentions for the upcoming day. These are tangible and defined outcomes that you seek to generate or bring about in your life on this particular day. Write these things down. Now, arise and proceed towards the fulfillment of your intentions. Please ensure that you constantly bear these tasks in your thoughts throughout the day to avoid any oversight in their timely completion.

• Identify the elements that you appreciate in your current circumstances and articulate your appreciation. The expression of appreciation possesses an inherent ability to profoundly transform one's life experience.

• The things you dedicate your attention to tend to expand, and your focused thoughts materialize in the physical realm. Direct your attention solely towards the favorable aspects and refrain from dwelling on any unfavorable matters. Irrespective of the circumstances that may arise today, it is imperative that you adhere to this methodology, as doing so will effectively enhance your self-esteem.

Negatives Thoughts

The presence of negativity is persistent and shows no sign of dissipating in the near future. It is a permanent presence, impervious to any potential efforts that could hinder its enduring existence. It will impede your progress, hinder your advancement, and significantly diminish your quality of life. You must demonstrate a readiness and capability to contemplate the manifestations of negativity in your life. The initial step towards this is to assess whether you exhibit tendencies of negativity.

Do not be disheartened in the event that you come to realize that you indeed possess negative qualities. If such is the case, there is no rationale for one to persist in a negative state over an extended period. There is no need for concern regarding any impediments holding you back or restraining you. You have the ability to acquire knowledge on how to effectively alleviate and conquer your thoughts. You have the ability to uncover strategies to effectively and promptly overcome detrimental thoughts, enabling you to foster a more optimistic mindset and truly leverage the power of positive thinking.

In essence, it is inherently natural for one to discover certain unfavorable characteristics or thoughts within oneself. It is important to acknowledge that being human entails such nuances, and it should be accepted without reservation. Nevertheless, it is imperative to bear in mind the following proposition: cultivating a positive mindset is achievable through conscious determination. The significance of maintaining a positive outlook cannot be underestimated, as one has the ability to cultivate it themselves. You have the capacity to acquire skills in regulating cognitive processes, enabling you to transform your overall mindset from pessimistic to optimistic.

What is Negative Thinking?

Negative thinking encompasses any type of thought that possesses an intrinsically pessimistic or unfavorable nature.

Negativity seldom yields productivity, as it diverts attention away from potential solutions and instead fixates on identifying problems. Consequently, negativity has a propensity to rapidly intensify and exacerbate the overall situation. If one indulges in contemplating past actions that should not have been taken, rather than focusing on present possibilities, it becomes challenging to progress efficiently due to excessive preoccupation with bygone events. This kind of thinking should largely be avoided as it is unproductive. Merely abstaining from a certain action should not be misconstrued as a genuine recognition or understanding of the proper course of action. You are effectively eliminating one of the infinite possibilities from your roster.

Negative thinking can manifest itself as sheer pessimism, exemplified by statements like "I failed to fulfill my obligations" or "Today is an exceptionally terrible day," wherein the underlying sentiment of the thought is entirely adverse. Furthermore, it may manifest as a complete lack of accuracy, mirroring a cognitive distortion. Indeed, subsequently, you will be provided with a comprehensive compilation of various cognitive distortions that individuals commonly succumb to. This will facilitate your ability to discern negative thoughts at their onset.

By harboring such pessimistic thoughts, you are permitting negativity to exert control over your existence. Once again, reflect upon the sequence of events you have observed thus far, which forms the fundamental basis of CBT (cognitive-behavioral therapy) in its entirety. The propagation of negativity occurs when it is introduced into any environment. Negativity has the characteristic of being harmful and easily transmissible; even aspects of one's own being that were previously devoid of negativity will swiftly encounter negativity if it is permitted to foment and permeate adjoining thoughts and emotions.

It is possible that you are familiar with the concept of negative thinking, yet it is likely that you disregarded it as you did not perceive it to be relevant to your personal circumstances. One day, an individual awakens and perceives that their existence lacks depth and excitement, and the presence of pessimistic thoughts, which they previously believed to be distant, are now ominously nearby. You extensively study and engage with various resources related to the matter, while making attempts at implementing the readily available remedies; however, none of these strategies prove to be truly effective. You desire an approach that is grounded in realism.

Begin by conducting a sincere evaluation of your pessimism. The following is a compilation of the prevailing components of pessimistic thought patterns. If any or all of the items mentioned strike a chord with you, please continue perusing the following content. You tend to have a pessimistic mindset. This book will facilitate your comprehension of the origins of negative thinking, along with the perpetuating factors that continue to provoke and maintain it. And it will provide an insight into the techniques by which you can actively influence your thoughts to align with an objective perception of reality, thereby facilitating a more harmonious, optimistic, and efficient way of living. Please allocate a period to carefully examine the list provided below and expand upon it as desired.

"You exhibit a propensity for negativity when:

Your propensity for excessive criticism and judgement, coupled with an unwavering belief in your infallibility, creates an unfavorable environment that renders it challenging for individuals to maintain companionship with you.

You possess a general disposition of cynicism towards life, and your thoughts are preoccupied and restrained by pessimistic contemplations of potential negative outcomes.

One's true potential in life remains unfulfilled due to a lack of trust and belief in one's ability to seize the exceptional opportunities that abound.

You are steadily growing more agitated, melancholic, and temperamental with an inability to derive any pleasure from your surroundings.

Your negativity about people and events is generally based on a gut feeling, honed over many years.

After conducting a thorough self-evaluation, you have identified numerous aspects of your life that you find unsatisfactory due to a prevailing sense of disempowerment and restriction.

Pessimistic thinking leads to individuals displaying negative traits.

The pessimistic thoughts harbored within your mind will undoubtedly contribute to the development of a cynical demeanor, leaving no room for uncertainty in this matter. Pessimism is an attribute that individuals can discern almost instantly during their interactions with others. If you perceive the individual with whom you are engaging as being inclined towards a pessimistic outlook, it is likely that there exists a valid rationale behind their disposition. Although they may purport to adopt a pragmatic perspective, it serves mainly as a rationalization for their inherently negative mindset during that specific juncture.

Ultimately, individuals with a pessimistic outlook on life are often dealing with personal challenges, causing them to perceive circumstances and thoughts from a negative standpoint. They are mechanically performing their duties, succumbing repeatedly to the influx of negativity in their lives, inundating every aspect of their actions, their speech, and their purpose for existence or engagement with the world. This issue frequently presents itself as a significant challenge. It is imperative to ascertain that individuals with a negative mindset often find themselves burdened by such thoughts, necessitating a transformation. In the upcoming chapter, we will commence our exploration of how negative thoughts and negativity can manifest. In the initial segment, we shall be delving into the prevailing cognitive patterns and their potential implications on relationships and cognitive processes.

It is important to bear in mind that harboring negativity is detrimental to one's well-being. It will not prove advantageous to you in any capacity. It will not facilitate your ability to effectively engage with the world. It will not aid in determining the utmost significance in life. It will not facilitate a sense of accomplishment or progress. Contrary to popular belief, it will actually have a detrimental impact on your progress. You will be miserable. You will be unhappy. You may encounter difficulties in interpersonal communication and experience a sense of personal distress as a result of your relationships and interactions. It is imperative for you to acquire the skills needed to overcome such obstacles and develop strategies to conquer negative thoughts.

Nevertheless, prior to overcoming the negativity, one must first attain an understanding of its presence. It is imperative that you acquire the knowledge required to effectively perceive the manner in which you engage with the world, in order to enhance your ability to adapt and manage it successfully. Once you have cultivated a heightened understanding of your actions, thought processes, and the underlying reasons for their prevalence, you will be poised to embark upon genuine and substantial strides towards fostering a positive outlook necessary for achieving success in your life.

Effective emotional management necessitates the synchrony of self-regulation and awareness of one's emotional state.
Self-regulation in emotional intelligence refers to the process of recognizing one's own emotions and effectively managing them. Self-control entails the conscious inhibition or modification of one's emotions, driven by the recognition that those emotions have the potential to result in personal or societal

maladaptation. The fact remains that emotions are complex entities that encompass both favorable and unfavorable aspects. We have the capacity to experience affection, which motivates us to engage in benevolent actions, while also having the potential to be consumed by anger, leading to actions that may be less beneficial.

Even matters of affection have the potential to compel individuals towards actions deemed detrimental or dissuaded. Emotions are complicated. Making alterations and maintaining a connection with things does not inherently signify our adherence to a course of action that yields a favorable outcome. It is a fact that there are occasions when it becomes essential to exert control over our emotions. Certainly, evaluating whether it is necessary to regulate one's emotions is a fundamental aspect of emotional self-awareness, just as comprehending the emotions of others is.

To effectively manage one's emotions, it is crucial to have a comprehensive comprehension of the consequences that arise from acting upon them. This could also be conceptualized as the logical consequence of your emotional state. Your emotional state may influence your decision-making, leading you to partake in actions that may yield personal benefits at the expense of others. Furthermore, allowing one's emotions to govern our actions may result in impulsive behavior, which often culminates in remorseful actions that we ultimately lament. By acknowledging your own emotions alongside self-management, you guarantee that you are conducting yourself in a manner that duly considers the impact of your behavior on others.

www.ingramcontent.com/pod-product-compliance
Lightning Source LLC
Chambersburg PA
CBHW050243120526
44590CB00016B/2198